IT'S TIME TO LEARN ABOUT BISON

It's Time to Learn about Bison

Walter the Educator

Silent King Books
A WhichHead Entertainment Imprint

Copyright © 2025 by Walter the Educator

All rights reserved. No part of this book may be reproduced in any manner whatsoever without written per- mission except in the case of brief quotations embodied in critical articles and reviews.

First Printing, 2024

Disclaimer

This book is a literary work; the story is not about specific persons, locations, situations, and/or circumstances unless mentioned in a historical context. Any resemblance to real persons, locations, situations, and/or circumstances is coincidental. This book is for entertainment and informational purposes only. The author and publisher offer this information without warranties expressed or implied. No matter the grounds, neither the author nor the publisher will be accountable for any losses, injuries, or other damages caused by the reader's use of this book. The use of this book acknowledges an understanding and acceptance of this disclaimer.

It's Time to Learn about Bison is a collectible early learning book by Walter the Educator suitable for all ages belonging to Walter the Educator's Time to Eat Book Series. Collect more books at WaltertheEducator.com

USE THE EXTRA SPACE TO TAKE NOTES AND DOCUMENT YOUR MEMORIES

BISON

Out on the plains so wide and free,

It's Time to Learn about

Bison

A mighty beast roams wild with glee.

With shaggy fur and shoulders high,

The bison walks beneath the sky.

Its coat is thick, both brown and bold,

To keep it warm when winds turn cold.

Through summer heat and winter snow,

The bison stays and continues to grow.

With hooves so strong, it pounds the ground,

A rumbling echo, a thundering sound.

In herds they gather, side by side,

Together strong, with strength and pride.

Its head is broad, its horns are stout,

To push and nudge or spin about.

It grazes grass from dusk till dawn,

Then moves along when food is gone.

It's Time to Learn about

Bison

Bison were once so great in number,

Roaming free without encumber.

But hunters came and took their space,

And left them few, a smaller race.

Now people help to bring them back,

Protect their homes and stop attack.

In parks they roam just like before,

Their mighty presence known once more.

A baby bison, small and bright,

Is called a calf, a lovely sight.

With reddish fur and eyes so wide,

It stays close by its mother's side.

Bison can run, and they can leap,

Though big and strong, they're quick on feet!

A sudden charge, a mighty dash,

It's Time to Learn about

Bison

They kick up dust and make a splash!

If ever you see one, stay away,

They need their space, just let them play!

Watch from afar, don't get too near,

Respect their home and show no fear.

So now you know, both big and small,

The bison's tale, its rise and fall.

A symbol strong, so brave and free,

It's Time to Learn about

Bison

A part of nature's history!

ABOUT THE CREATOR

Walter the Educator is one of the pseudonyms for Walter Anderson. Formally educated in Chemistry, Business, and Education, he is an educator, an author, a diverse entrepreneur, and he is the son of a disabled war veteran. "Walter the Educator" shares his time between educating and creating. He holds interests and owns several creative projects that entertain, enlighten, enhance, and educate, hoping to inspire and motivate you. Follow, find new works, and stay up to date with Walter the Educator™ at WaltertheEducator.com

www.ingramcontent.com/pod-product-compliance
Lightning Source LLC
LaVergne TN
LVHW052017060526
838201LV00059B/4073